FRETBOARD ROADMAPS COUNTRY GUITAR

THE ESSENTIAL GUITAR PATTERNS THAT ALL THE PROS KNOW AND USE

BY FRED SOKOLOW

The Recording

Guitar and Vocals—Fred Sokolow

Sound Engineer and Other Instruments—Denis O'Hanlon

Recorded at O'Hanlon Recording and Music Services

ISBN 978-0-634-00139-4

HAL•LEONARD®
CORPORATION

7777 W. BLUEMOUND RD. P.O. BOX 13819 MILWAUKEE, WI 53213

Visit Hal Leonard Online at
www.halleonard.com

CONTENTS

INTRODUCTION

Accomplished country guitarists—electric and acoustic—can ad lib hot solos and play backup in any key—all over the fretboard. They know several different soloing approaches and can choose the style that fits the tune, whether it's vintage honky tonk, hard driving country-rock, or a pretty ballad with pop changes.

There are moveable patterns on the guitar fretboard that make it easy to do these things. The pros are aware of these "fretboard roadmaps," even if they don't read music. If you want to jam with other players, this is essential guitar knowledge.

You need the fretboard roadmaps if...

► All your soloing sounds the same and you want some different styles and flavors from which to choose.

► Some keys are harder to play in than others.

► Your guitar fretboard beyond the 5th fret is mysterious, uncharted territory.

► You can't automatically play any familiar melody.

► You know a lot of "bits and pieces" on the guitar, but you don't have a system that ties it all together.

Read on, and many mysteries will be explained. If you're serious about playing country guitar, the pages that follow can shed light and save you a great deal of time.

Good luck,

Fred Sokolow

This book is a country guitarist's extension of Fred Sokolow's *Fretboard Roadmaps* **(Hal Leonard Corporation, HL00696514), which includes even more music theory for guitarists, along with musical examples, solos and licks. We urge you to use** *Fretboard Roadmaps* **as a reference, along with** *Fretboard Roadmaps for the Country Guitarist.*

THE RECORDING AND THE PRACTICE TRACKS

All the licks, riffs and tunes in this book are played on the accompanying CD.

There are also five practice tracks on the recording. Each one has a standard country groove and progression. They are mixed so that the lead guitar is on one side of your stereo and the backup band is on the other.

Each track contains a standard progression and illustrates the use of certain scales, chords, techniques or licks.

You can also tune out the lead guitar track and use the backup tracks to practice playing solos.

◆ #1 NOTES ON THE FRETBOARD

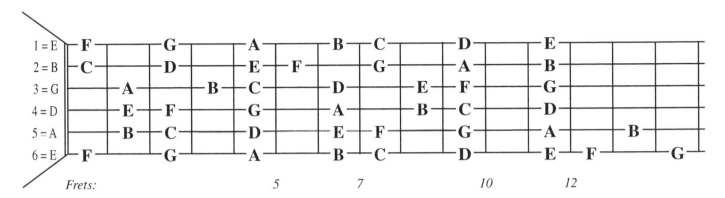

1 = E	F		G		A		B	C		D		E	
2 = B	C		D		E	F		G		A		B	
3 = G		A		B	C		D		E	F		G	
4 = D		E	F		G		A		B	C		D	
5 = A		B	C		D		E	F		G		A	B
6 = E	F		G		A		B	C		D		E	F	G

Frets: 5   7   10   12

WHY?

▶ Knowing where the notes are (especially the notes on the 6th and 5th strings) will help you find chords and scales up and down the neck. It will help you alter and understand chords (e.g., *How do I flat the seventh in this chord? Why is this chord minor instead of major?*). It's a first step toward understanding music.

WHAT?

▶ *The notes get higher in pitch as you go up the alphabet and up the fretboard.*

▶ *A whole step is two frets, and a half step is one fret.*

▶ *Sharps are one fret higher:* 6th string/3rd fret = G, so 6th string/4th fret = G♯. 6th string/8th fret = C, so 6th string/9th fret = C♯.

▶ *Flats are one fret lower:* 6th string/5th fret = A, so 6th string/4th fret = A♭; 6th string/10th fret = D, so 6th string/9th fret = D♭.

HOW?

▶ *Fretboard markings help.* Most guitars have fretboard inlays or marks somewhere on the neck indicating the 5th, 7th, 10th and 12th frets. Become aware of these signposts.

DO IT!

▶ *Start by memorizing the notes on the 6th and 5th strings.* You will need to know these notes very soon–for Roadmap #3.

SUMMING UP—NOW YOU KNOW...

▶ *The location of the notes on the fretboard*

▶ *The meaning of these musical terms:*

whole step, half step, sharp (♯), flat (♭)

#2 THE MAJOR SCALE

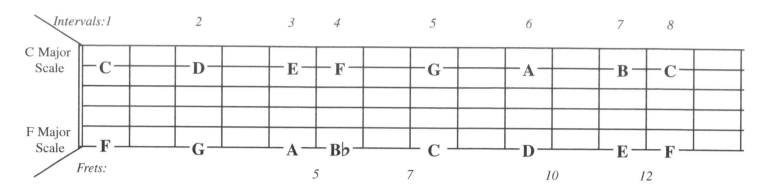

WHY?

▶ To understand music and to communicate with other players, you need to know about the major scale. The major scale is a ruler that helps you measure distances between notes and chords. Knowing the major scale will help you understand and talk about chord construction, scales and chord relationships.

WHAT?

▶ *The major scale is the "Do-Re-Mi" scale you have heard all your life.* Countless familiar tunes are composed of notes from this scale.

▶ *Intervals are distances between notes.* The intervals of the major scale are used to describe these distances. For example, E is the third note of the C major scale, and it is four frets above C (see above). This distance is called a *third*. Similarly, A is a third above F, and C♯ is a third above A. On the guitar, *a third is always a distance of four frets.*

HOW?

▶ *Every major scale has the same interval pattern of whole and half-steps:*

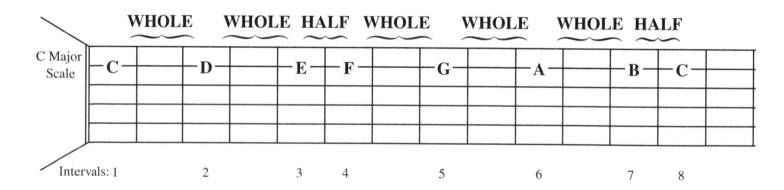

In other words, the major scale ascends and descends by whole steps (two frets at a time) with two exceptions: there is a half step (one fret) from the third to the fourth notes and from the seventh to the eighth notes. It's helpful to think of intervals in terms of frets (e.g., a third is 4 frets).

► *Intervals can extend above the octave.** They correspond to lower intervals: a 2nd above the octave is called a *9th,* a 4th above the octave is an *11th,* and so on:

C Major Scale

Intervals:

1	2	3	4	5	6	7	8	9	10	11	12	13

C — D — E — F — G — A — B — C — D — E — F — G — A

Frets: 5   7   10   12   15   17   20

DO IT!

► *Learn the major scale intervals* on one string by playing any note and finding the note that is a second (two frets) higher, a third (four frets) higher, and so on:

SUMMING UP — NOW YOU KNOW...

► *The intervals of the major scale and the number of frets that make up each interval*

* An "octave" is the interval between the 1st and 8th note of a major scale. An octave above C is a higher C note.

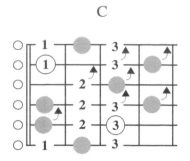

C

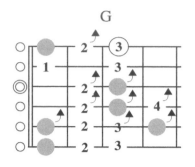

G

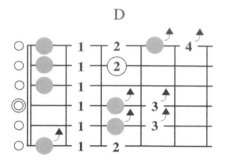

D

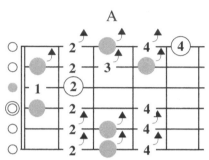

A

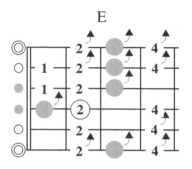

E

○ =play the string unfretted

WHY?

▶ Each key has its own major scale, which is used for playing melodies and licks. Many classic country solos were based on first position scales, and modern pickers use them more than ever.

WHAT?

▶ *Every key has its own scale and characteristic licks.* You only use the C scale to play in the key of C, the E scale to play in E, and so on.

▶ *Each scale (and the licks that go with it) can be played throughout a tune,* in spite of chord changes within the tune.

▶ *The root notes in each scale are circled.* The numbers are suggested fingerings.

▶ *The grey circles in each scale are "blue notes,"* flatted 3rds, 5ths, and 7ths. They add a bluesy flavor to the scales.

▶ *The numbers are fingering suggestions:* "1" means "index finger"; "2" means "middle finger," and so on.

▶ *The scale notes with bends* $(2^\nearrow, 3^\nearrow)$ *can be stretched or choked.* This left-hand technique, in which you pull a string up or down with your fretting finger to raise its pitch, is a very important blues sound.

8

HOW?

► *Put your hand "in position" for each scale by fingering the appropriate chord* (e.g., play an E chord to get in position for the E major scale). You don't have to maintain the chord while playing the scale, but it's a reference point.

► *Play "up and down" each scale (as written below) until it feels comfortable and familiar.* Play the chord before playing the scale, and "loop" the scale—play it several times in a row, with no pause between repetitions. Here are the five scales to practice:

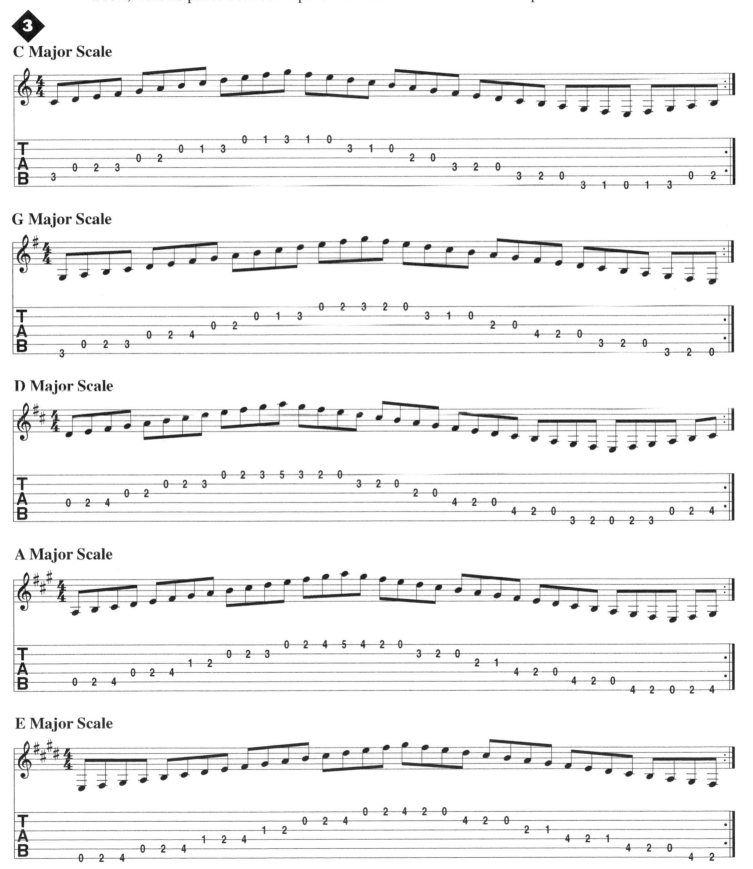

3

C Major Scale

G Major Scale

D Major Scale

A Major Scale

E Major Scale

DO IT!

► The following solos show how to use all five major scales to play some classic licks. All five make use of the basic I-IV-V, 8-bar format described in **ROADMAPS #4 AND #6**. They feature lots of bluesy string-bending.

Key of C

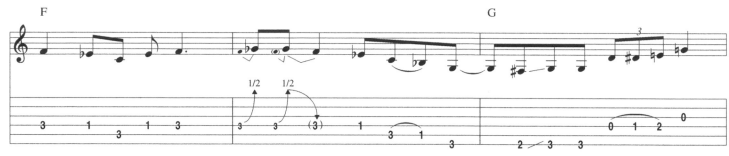

Key of G

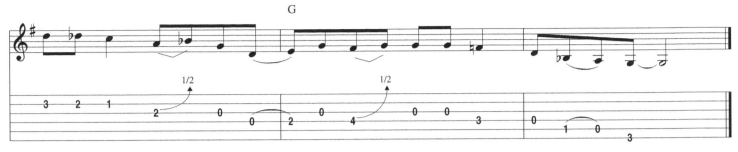

Key of D

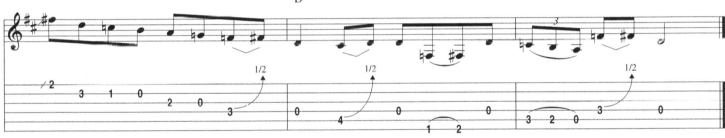

Key of A

Key of E

SUMMING UP—NOW YOU KNOW...

► *How to play five first-position major scales* (C, G, D, A and E) *and how to use them to play licks and solos*

► *How to stretch strings for a bluesy effect*

► *The meaning of the musical term "blue notes," and how to add them to your major scales and licks*

#4 TWO MOVEABLE MAJOR CHORDS

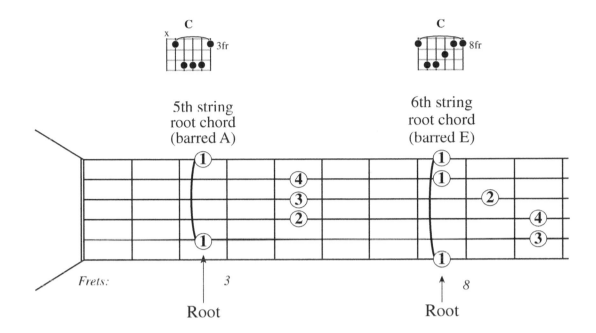

WHY?

► Moveable chords have no open (unfretted) strings, so they can be played (moved) all over the fretboard. The two moveable chords of **ROADMAP #4** will get you started playing chords up and down the neck. They help you play in any key without using a capo.

WHAT?

► A *chord* is a group of three or more notes played simultaneously.

► A *moveable chord* can be played all over the fretboard. It contains no open (unfretted) strings.

► A *root* is the note that gives a chord its name.

HOW?

► *The 6th string identifies the 6th-string root/barred E chord.* It's a G chord when played at the 3rd fret, because the 6th string/3rd fret is G. At the 6th fret it's a B♭ chord, and so on.

► *The 5th string identifies the 5th-string root/barred A chord.* It's a C chord at the 3rd fret, because the 5th string/3rd fret is C. At the 9th fret it's F♯ (G♭), and so on.

DO IT!

► *Play the 6th-string root chords all over the fretboard*, naming the chords as you play them.

► *Play the 5th-string root chords all over the fretboard* and name them.

► *Play this country progression* using 6th string root chords.* It matches "I'm Thinking Tonight of My Blue Eyes," "Wild Side of Life," "Tiger By the Tail," "Wabash Cannonball," "Walking the Floor Over You," "Your Cheatin' Heart" and many more classic country tunes.

* A *progression* is a repeated chord sequence.

This progression is divided into *bars*, with four beats (strums) to a bar. The repeat signs ‖: :‖ tell you to repeat the eight bars of music, or any music enclosed within them. This repeat sign ╱ means play the same chord as in the previous bar.

▶ *Play the same progression using 5th string root chords.*

Key of G

▶ *Play it in different keys.* This is easy if you observe the fret-distances (intervals) between chords.

▷ For example, the second chord (C) in the progression is five frets above the first chord (G). This is true in all keys.

▷ The third chord (D) is two frets above the second chord. This is true in any key.

Key of F

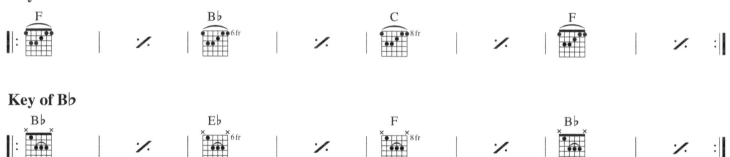

Key of B♭

▶ *Power Chords:* Modern country guitarists have borrowed rock's *power chords*—abbreviated versions of the two moveable major chords of **ROADMAP #4.** The resulting two- or three-note chords have a "5" in their name (G5, C5) because they consist of a root and a fifth, but no third.

► **Boogie Licks:** Chuck Berry popularized a blues-boogie lick, built on power chords, that has become a staple in rock and country backup guitar. Play this example, then move it up and down the fretboard and play it in other keys:

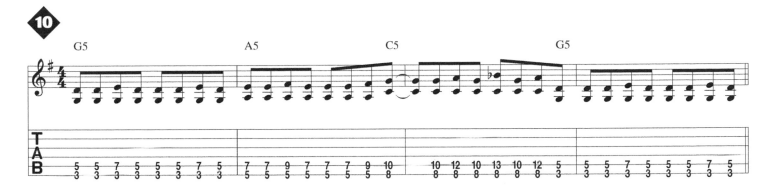

Here's another boogie lick. This one uses 5th string root chords:

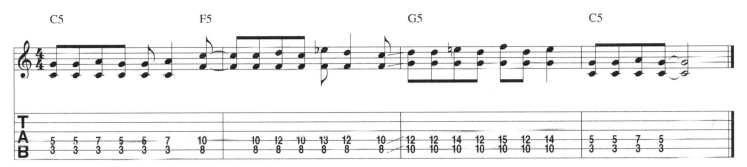

SUMMING UP—NOW YOU KNOW...

► *How to play any major chord two ways:* with a 6th string root and with a 5th string root

► *How to play a basic country progression in all keys*

► *How to play 6th and 5th string root power chords*

► *How to use power chords to play boogie licks*

► *The meaning of these musical terms:*

Chord, Moveable Chord, Root, Power Chord, Boogie Lick, Progression

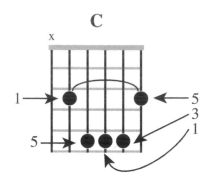

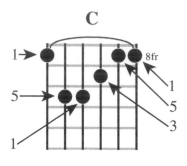

WHY?

▶ You can play dozens of chords (minors, sevenths, major sevenths, etc.) by altering slightly the two basic, moveable major chords of **ROADMAP #4**. For example, you can play one fret lower on one string to make a major chord minor. This is an easy way to expand your chord vocabulary.

WHAT?

▶ *The two moveable major chords (and all major chords) consist of roots, 3rds and 5ths.* Make sure you know the intervals in these two formations. The chord grids above **ROADMAP #5** identify the intervals (e.g., the 5th and 2nd strings in the barred E formation are 5ths).

▶ *You can relate other intervals (4ths, 7ths, etc.) to the intervals you already know:* A 4th is one fret higher than a 3rd, and a 6th is two frets higher than a 5th.

HOW?

▶ *Compare every new chord you learn to a basic chord you already know.* Every small chord grid in the "DO IT" section that follows is a variation of a basic chord formation.

DO IT!

▶ *Here are the most-played chords.* Play them and compare each formation to the larger grid to the left, from which it is derived.

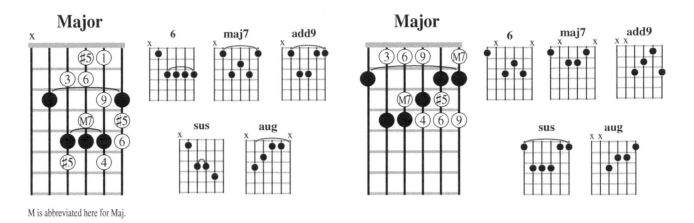

M is abbreviated here for Maj.

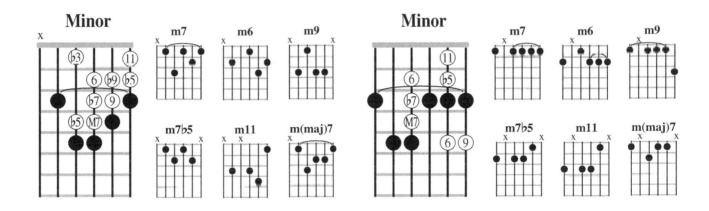

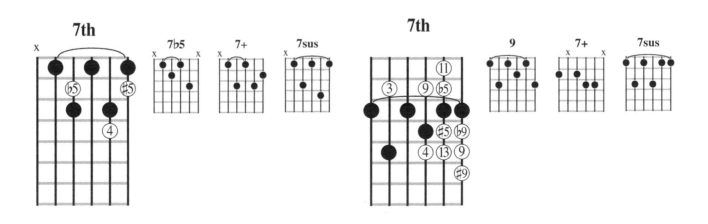

Here is another very useful seventh shape with a 5th string root.

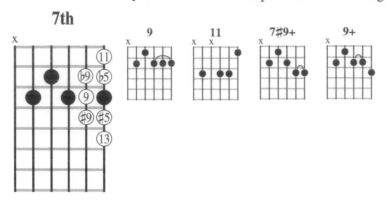

Diminished chords are seventh chords with a ♭3rd, ♭5th and ♭♭7th.

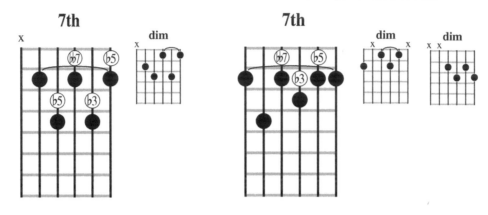

SUMMING UP—NOW YOU KNOW...

▶ *Two ways to play many chord types*—with a 5th string root and a 6th string root

THE I—IV—V CHORD FAMILIES

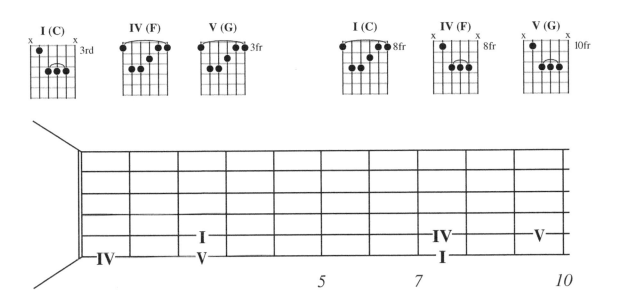

I (C)   IV (F)   V (G)   I (C)   IV (F)   V (G)

WHY?

▶ *I–IV–V chord family* is the basis for countless country chord progressions. This roadmap shows how to find the I-IV-V family automatically, in any key, all over the fretboard.

WHAT?

▶ *The Roman numerals in the chart above are the roots of the I, IV and V chords in the key of C.*

▶ *The numbers I, IV and V refer to the major scale of your key.*

HOW?

▶ *The I-IV-V root patterns in the fretboard chart are moveable.*

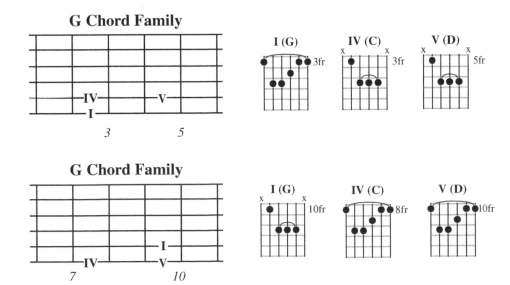

G Chord Family

I (G)   IV (C)   V (D)

G Chord Family

I (G)   IV (C)   V (D)

▶ *Variations of the two moveable major chords can be used in the chord family.* Country tunes often include seventh or ninth chords, instead of major chords. There are also minor key songs, in which the I and IV chords, or all three chords, are minors, or minor 7ths. *Regardless of these variations, the I-IV-V root relationships are the same.* Here are some sample chord families. They are all in the key of G and all roots are white:

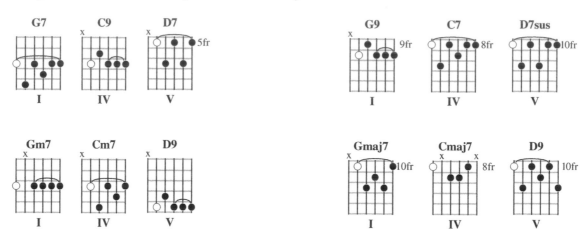

DO IT!

▶ *Play the basic I-IV-V progression from* **ROADMAP 4** *in several keys,* first with a 6th string root/I chord, then with a 5th string root/I chord:

11

Key of F:

Key of C:

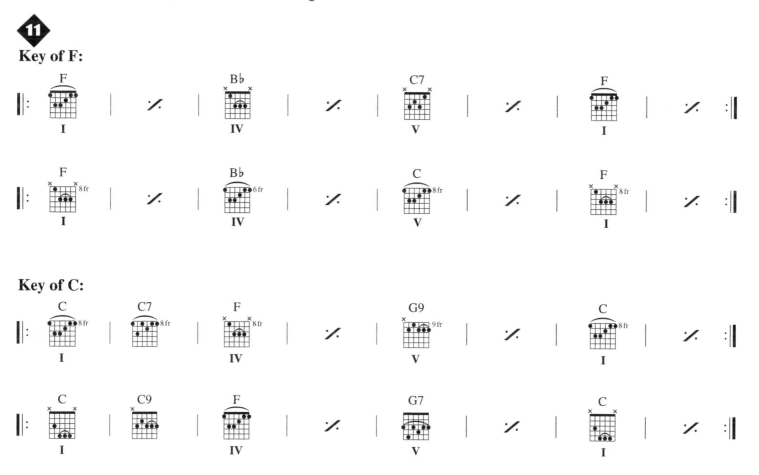

20

► *Play the basic I-IV-I-V progression in several keys,* with a 6th string root/I chord and with a 5th string root/I chord. Many songs are based on it, including "Act Naturally," "Faded Love," "Green, Green Grass of Home," the verse of "I Can't Stop Loving You," "Satin Sheets," "Crazy Arms," "Blue Moon of Kentucky," and more.

Key of C:

► Play the 12-bar blues progression in several keys. It's the basis of many country classics, such as "T for Texas," "I'm Movin' On," "Move It on Over," "Folsom Prison Blues," "Honky Tonk Blues" and more. Here it is in A:

Key of A:

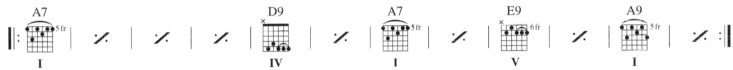

SUMMING UP—NOW YOU KNOW...

► *Two different ways to play the I–IV–V chord family—in any key*: with a 6th string root/I chord and with a 5th string root/I chord

► *How to play common I–IV–V country progressions, including the 12-bar blues, in any key, two ways*

► *How to use chord variations within the I–IV–V chord families*

► *The meaning of these musical terms:*

I Chord, IV Chord, V Chord, Chord Family, 12-Bar Blues

#7 THE F—D—A ROADMAP

F
F formation

F
D formation

F
A formation

All F Chords:

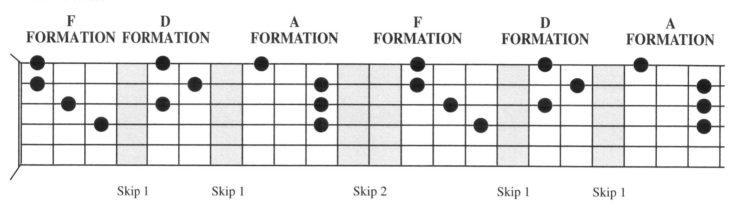

| F FORMATION | D FORMATION | A FORMATION | F FORMATION | D FORMATION | A FORMATION |

Skip 1   Skip 1   Skip 2   Skip 1   Skip 1

WHY?

▶ The *"F–D–A" Roadmap* shows you how to play any major chord all over the fretboard, using three major chord formations.

WHAT?

▶ The chords in the fretboard diagram above are all F chords.

HOW?

▶ *To memorize this roadmap,* remember: *F-SKIP 1, D-SKIP 1, A-SKIP 2.* In other words, play an F formation, skip a fret, play a D formation, skip a fret; play an A formation, skip two frets.

▶ Use the F-D-A roadmap to play all the D chords:

All D Chords:

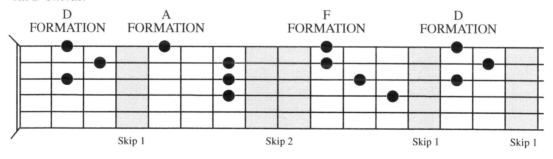

| D FORMATION | A FORMATION | F FORMATION | D FORMATION |

Skip 1   Skip 2   Skip 1   Skip 1

▶ Notice that you can climb the fretboard *starting with any chord formation.* The F–D–A roadmap is a continuous loop that you can enter at any point. It can be the D–A–F or A–F–D roadmap. The "skips" are always the same: one skip after F, one after D, two after A.

DO IT!

▶ *Play the following solo to the old country standard "Wabash Cannonball." It consists of ascending and descending chord fragments.*

▶ *Play a solo to the same tune, using arpeggios.* This creates a fingerpicking sound. (To play an arpeggio, pick each of the notes of a chord separately, going up or down in pitch.)

► *You can alter the three major chord formations to create 6ths,7ths, add9 and suspended chords.* This allows you to get more variety out of your F–D–A roadmap. Here are the altered chord shapes, and yet another "Wabash Cannonball" solo that shows how to use them:

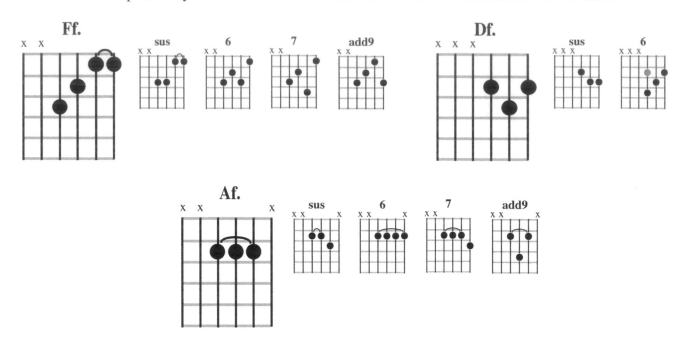

Wabash Cannonball—With Altered Chords

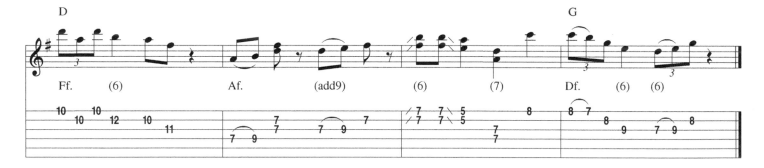

SUMMING UP—NOW YOU KNOW...

► *How to play three major chord fragments*

► *How to use them to play any major chord all over the fretboard* (with the F–D–A roadmap)

► *How to alter them to create 6ths, 7ths, add9 and suspended chords*

► *How to play moveable country licks and solos, based on chord fragments*

► *The meaning of the musical term "arpeggio"*

24

#8 CHORD FRAGMENTS/CHORD FAMILIES

Three B♭ Chord Families

● = I   ○ = IV   ◐ = V

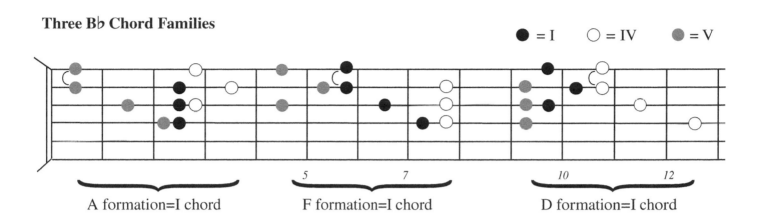

A formation=I chord   F formation=I chord   D formation=I chord

WHY?

▶ This chart arranges the three chord fragments of **ROADMAP #7** into chord families to help you play chords and chord-based licks all over the fretboard *in any key.*

WHAT?

▶ *You can play at least three chord families for every key,* as shown above.

HOW?

▶ *Learn the relationships of the three chord fragment/chord families* and you can make quick chord changes automatically. For example, if you're playing a I chord with an F formation, the IV chord is the A formation on the same three frets.

DO IT!

▶ *This solo to a standard I–IV–V progression will give you some practice memorizing the chord family relationships.*

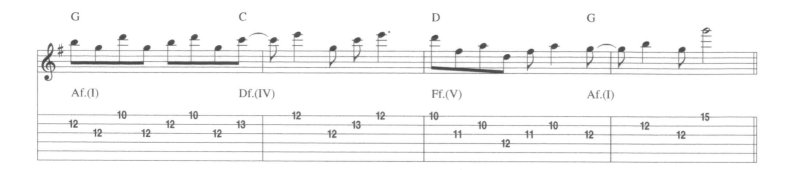

▶ In this I–IV–I–V progression, the lead guitar makes use of all three key-of-C chord fragment/chord families. The chord-licks include slides, *hammer-ons* and *pull-offs* that add *6ths, suspended 4ths* and *add 9ths* to the major chord fragments.

▷ To play a hammer-on, sound a note by fretting a string suddenly with your fretting finger.

▷ To play a pull-off, sound a note by plucking downward on a string.

SUMMING UP — NOW YOU KNOW...

▶ *How to locate three different chord families for any key, using chord fragments*

▶ *How to play many licks, strums and arpeggios, using all three chord fragment/chord families*

#9 THREE MOVEABLE BLUES BOXES

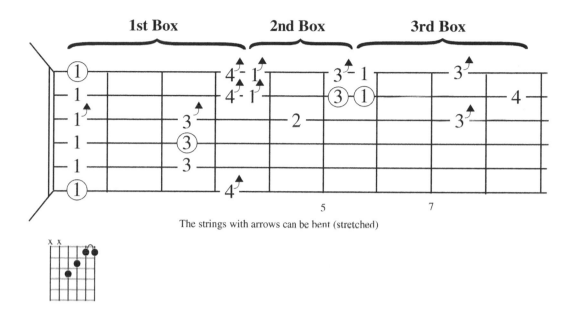

The strings with arrows can be bent (stretched)

WHY?

▶ The moveable scales of this **ROADMAP**, often called blues boxes, are the basis for modern blues and rock guitar, and they are often used in country music.

WHAT?

▶ *The three blues boxes above are F blues scales.* The root notes are circled. The numbers indicate suggested fingering positions.

▶ *Often, you can solo in one blues box throughout a song, in spite of chord changes.*

▶ *The blues boxes are pentatonic*, which means they contain five notes. However, you can add other notes and still sound bluesy.

F Blues Scale with "Extra Notes"

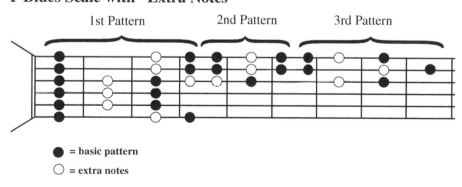

● = basic pattern

○ = extra notes

HOW?

▶ *To put your left hand in position for the first blues box, play an F formation at the appropriate fret.* For the key of G, play an F formation at the third fret, which is a G chord.

27

First Box, Key of G

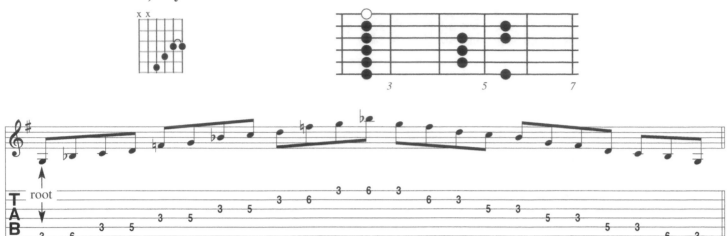

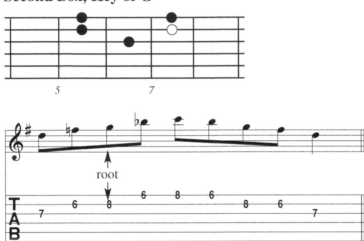

► *To put your left hand in position for the second blues box, play the root note on the second string with your third (ring) finger.* In G, play the G note on the 2nd string/8th fret with your ring finger.

Second Box, Key of G

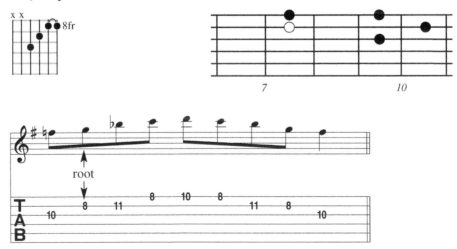

► *To put your left hand in position for the third blues box, play the F formation of the IV chord.*

Third Box, Key of G

28

DO IT!

▶ *Play the following blues box licks:*

First Box, Key of G

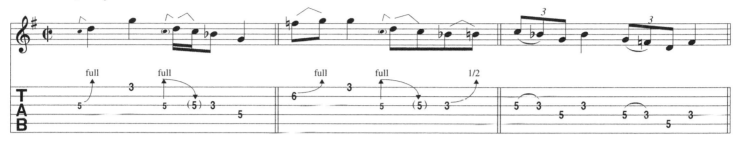

Second Box, Key of G

Sliding from Second to First box

Third Box, Key of G

▶ *Use the blues boxes to solo on bluesy tunes.* Although blues box licks sound inappropriate on many country tunes, pretty ballads and songs with "pop" chord changes, they fit the honky-tonk genre. Blues licks clash with Roy Acuff's gospel classic, "The Great Speckled Bird," but they work well in Buck Owens' "Tiger by the Tail," which has exactly the same chord progression.

The following solo illustrates the use of all three key-of-A blues boxes in a typical I–IV–I–V country progression. They give the tune an unmistakable honky-tonk feel:

Honky Tonk #1

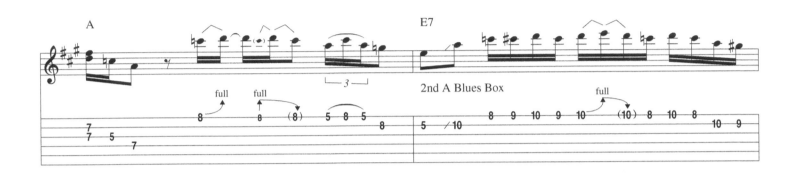

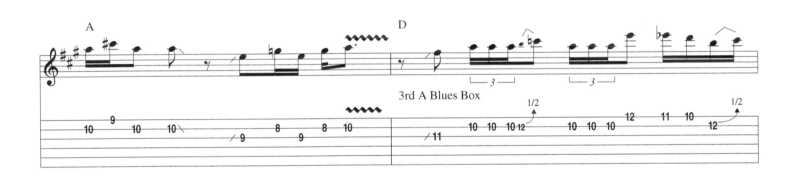

► *Often, the third blues box works well in non-bluesy tunes,* where the first and second boxes sound inappropriate. "The Water Is Wide," below, has a contemporary country ballad feel. It's in G, and the solo consists of third blues box G licks.

The Water Is Wide

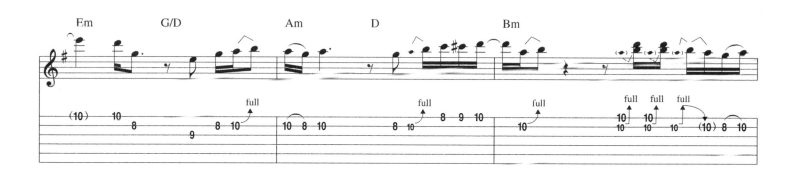

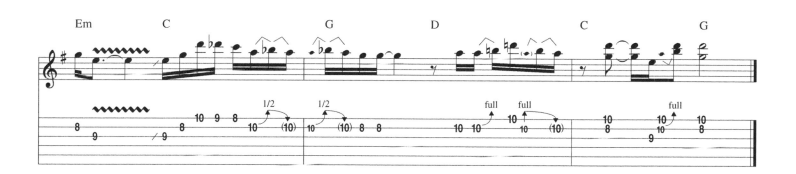

► *Relative minor blues scale substitution:* When a song does not call for a bluesy feel, you can still use the first and second blues boxes—just play them *three frets lower than the song's actual key.* For example, the following version of "Chilly Winds" is in the key of C, and the solo makes use of first and second A blues boxes. The song is an old blues that has been performed by many country, bluegrass and rock artists.

Chilly Winds

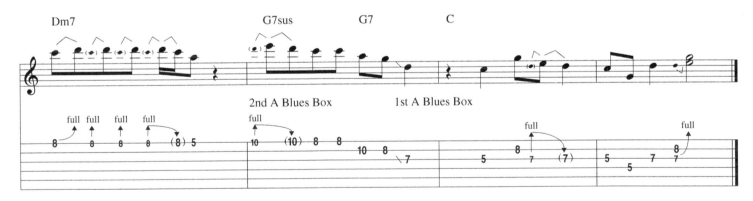

SUMMING UP—NOW YOU KNOW...

▶ *Three moveable blues boxes*

▶ *Many licks that go with each box*

▶ *How to use the boxes to improvise single-note solos in any key*

▶ *How to substitute the relative minor blues scale when blues boxes don't fit in a tune*

#10 MAJOR PENTATONIC SCALES

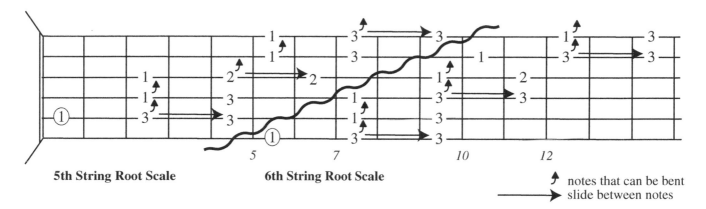

5th String Root Scale   **6th String Root Scale**

↗ notes that can be bent
→ slide between notes

WHY?

▶ These two versatile scales are important to any country lead guitarist. They're useful in country ballads, honky-tonk tunes, Southern rock, country rock, and pop tunes with many chord changes. They are the basis of single-note and double-note solos and licks, including "steel licks," in which the guitar imitates a pedal steel.

WHAT?

▶ There are two B♭ scales in **ROADMAP #10**. *One has a 6th string root, the other a 5th string root.* Both roots are circled.

▶ *The long arrows indicate slides, short arrows can be stretched (choked).*

▶ *Often, one sliding scale can be played throughout a tune.* If a tune is in the key of C, you can use C sliding scales throughout.

▶ *You can also "go with the changes"* and use the sliding scale that matches each chord change, especially when a song stays on a chord for more than a few bars.

▶ *The major pentatonic scale contains these five notes: 1, 2, 3, 5 and 6.* In the key of C, that's: C(1), D(2), E(3), G(5), A(6).

HOW?

▶ *Play both sliding scales over and over to become familiar with them.*

5th String Root/B♭ Sliding Scale

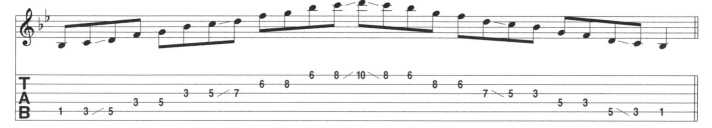

6th String Root/B♭ Sliding Scale

DO IT!

► *Play the following solo to a key-of-C, I–IV–V tune.* It consists of C sliding scales and has a honky-tonk feel.

Honky Tonk #2

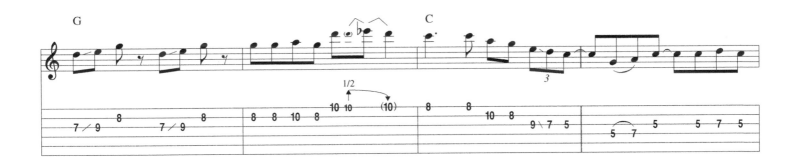

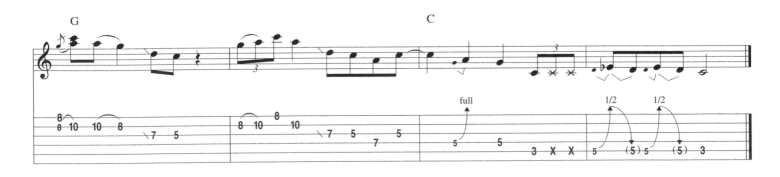

34

► *The following solo goes "with the changes."* It has the same chord progression as the last solo, but the lead guitarist uses the F sliding scale during the F chord, and the G sliding scale during the G chord.

Honky Tonk #3

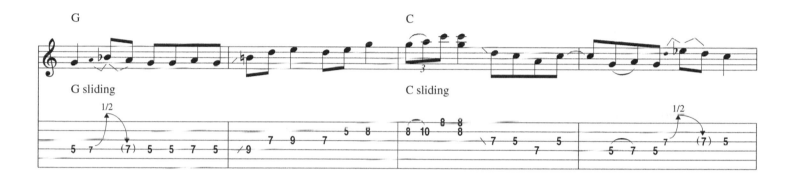

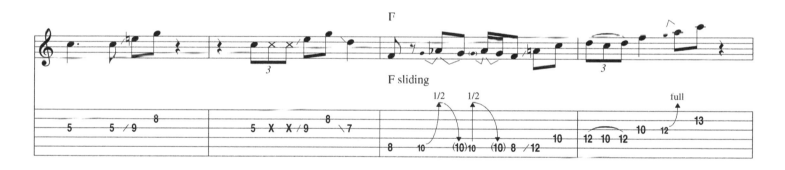

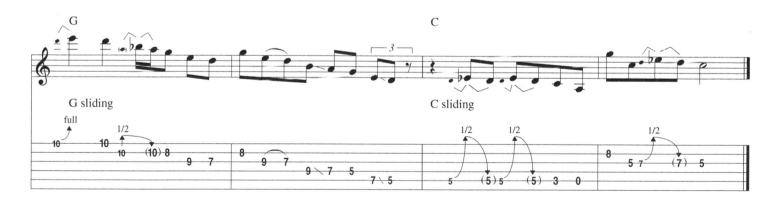

► *"Double-stop" sliding licks have a raunchy, Southern rock sound.* Play the following licks, in which you bend the second or fourth note of the pentatonic scale while holding a higher note:

G Sliding Scale—6th String Root

C Sliding Scale—5th String Root

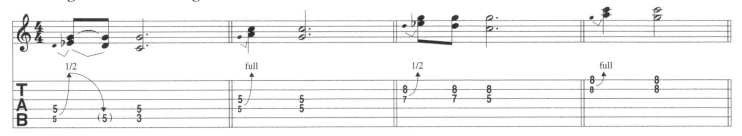

▶ *Play the following country rock version of the old blues, "See See Rider." It includes a lot of "double-stop" sliding scale licks:*

See See Rider

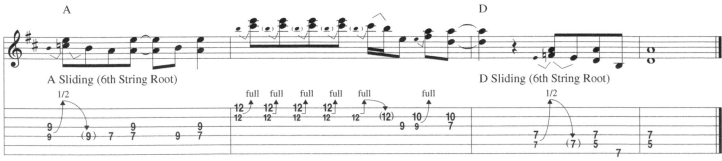

► *Play the following "steel licks," and use them in the honky-tonk version of "See See Rider"
that follows.* These single-note variations of the above double-note licks imitate the twangy,
country sound of a pedal steel.

G Sliding Scale—6th String Root   **C Sliding Scale—5th String Root**

See See Rider with Steel Licks

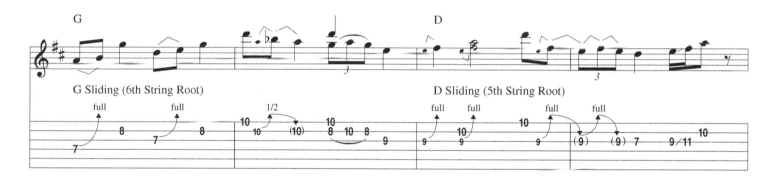

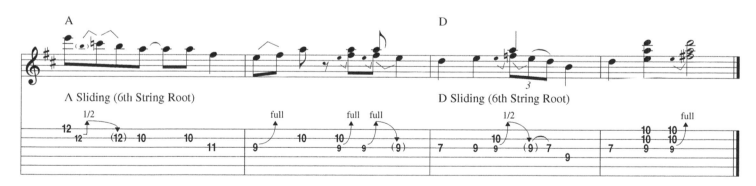

SUMMING UP—NOW YOU KNOW...

► *Two sliding pentatonic scales for each key and how to use them for soloing*

► *A group of double-note licks based on the sliding scales*

► *Several "steel licks" based on the sliding scales*

◆ #11 ◆ A MOVEABLE DOUBLE-NOTE LICK

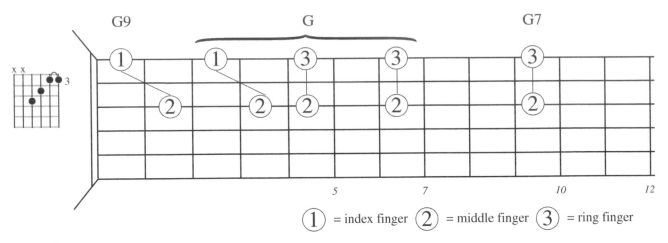

① = index finger ② = middle finger ③ = ring finger

WHY?

▶ This moveable double-note pattern opens up a whole "bag of licks." It's the basis for many licks and solos, including the famous "blue yodel" lick.

WHAT?

▶ *"Home base" for this series of licks is the F formation.* To play A licks, position your fretting hand at the fifth fret/F formation.

▶ *There are countless double-note licks* that spring from this roadmap. They can go up, down, or up and down, as shown by these variations on an A chord:

28

Blue Yodel

▶ *These licks can be played as backup fills, during solos, and as "riffs."* (repetitious signature licks that give a tune a distinct character).

▶ *The G9 and G7* (above and below the three bracketed notes in **ROADMAP #11**) *offer still more variations.* See examples in the "DO IT" section.

HOW?

▶ *Change F formations with the tune's chord changes:* When there is a C chord, play double-note licks based on the F formation/C chord at the 8th fret.

▶ *You can start a lick at any of the five positions of* **ROADMAP #11**—not just at the F formation.

DO IT!

► *Use the double-note licks as fills and in solos.* The following country-rock version of "Careless Love" features double-note fills during the singing and a solo that consists almost entirely of double-note licks.

Careless Love

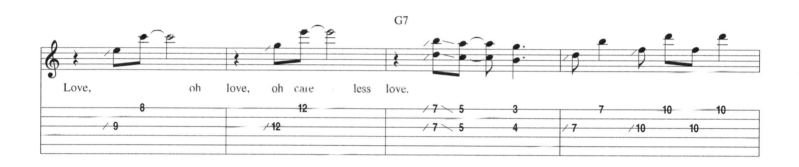

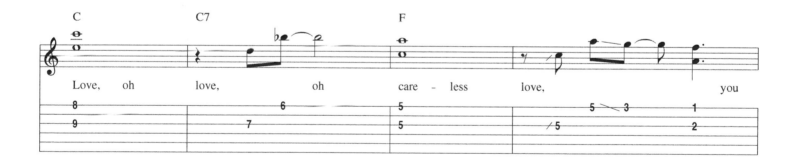

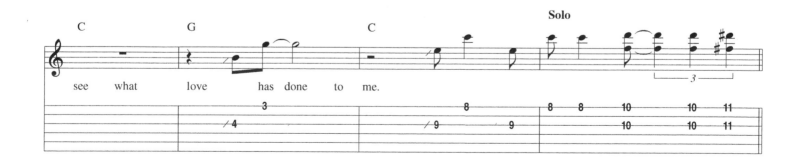

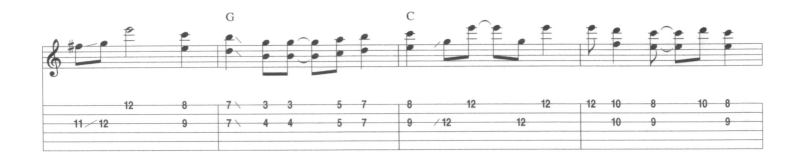

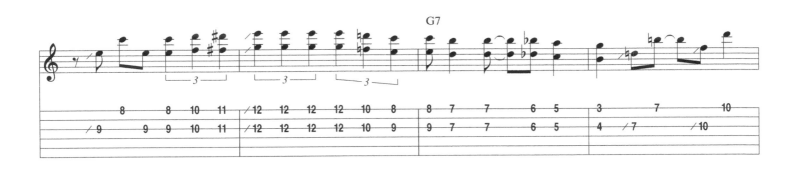

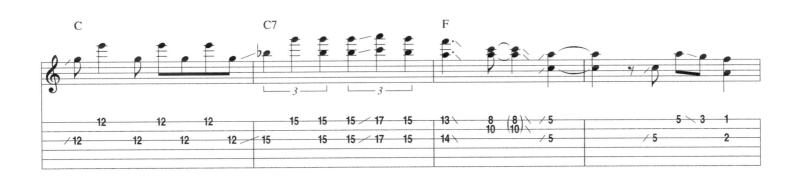

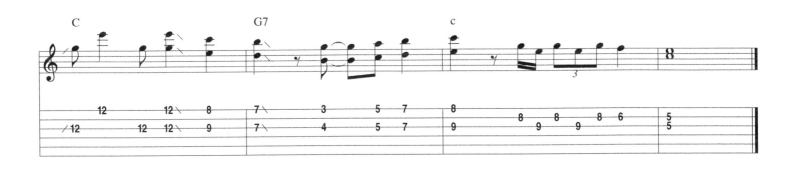

► *"Stagolee," below, features double-note fills. Notice how the tonic 7th position (A7, bar 4) leads to the IV chord (D).* The 9th position also "leads up a fourth," as illustrated in bars 9-10: The E9 position leads to A.

Stagolee

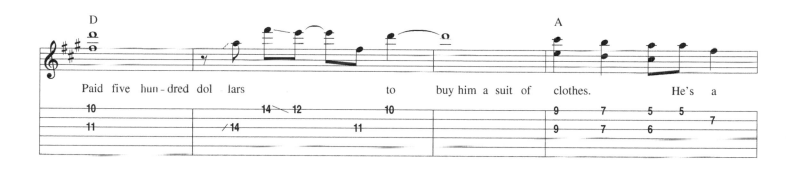

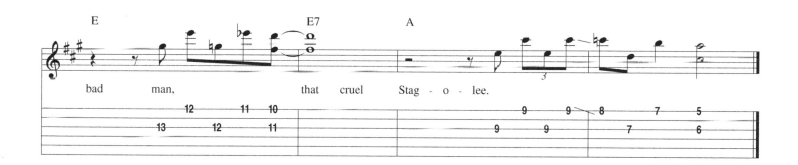

SUMMING UP—NOW YOU KNOW...

► *How to play a series of double-note licks on the 1st and 3rd strings for solos or backup, in any key*

► *How to play the "blue yodel" lick*

► *That 7th or 9th chords often lead "up a fourth"*

#12 MOVEABLE MAJOR SCALES

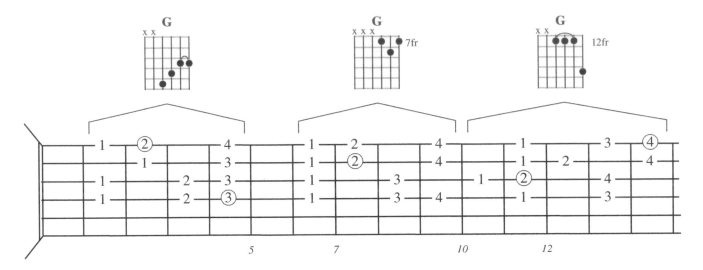

WHY?

▶ *Countless country melodies are based on the major scale.* Familiarity with several move-able major scales allows you to find and play melodies without memorizing them in advance. It brings you a step closer to any player's goal: to be able to play whatever you can hear.

WHAT?

▶ *The numbers on the fretboard in* **ROADMAP #12** *are left-hand fingering suggestions.*

▶ *The three scales of* **ROADMAP #12** *are based on the three chord fragments* of **ROADMAPS #7** and **8.** The root notes (all G's in this diagram) are circled. Play the appropriate chord frag-ment to get your fretting hand "in position" to play one of the major scales. For example, play an F formation at the 3rd fret to play the lowest G scale of **ROADMAP #12.**

HOW?

▶ *Here are the three G scales that match the three G chord fragments.* Play the chord frag-ment before playing the scale. Start each scale with its root note so you can recognize the "do-re-mi" sound you have heard all your life!

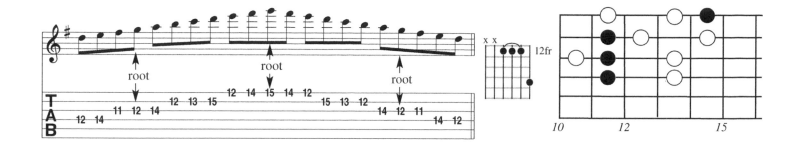

DO IT!

▶ *Become familiar with the scale patterns.* Use the F-formation scale pattern to play G, A, C, D and E major scales. Use the D formation pattern to play E, F, G and A major scales, and so on.

▶ *Use major scales to jam.* The following solo to the old country tune "Redwing" makes use of three G major scales, and includes some useful scale exercises:

Redwing

► *Use the major scales to play melodic solos.* "Careless Love," below, shows how to embellish a solo with string bends (bending up to the melody note from one or two frets back), slides and double-note licks.

Careless Love

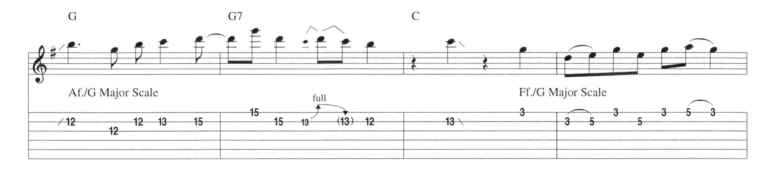

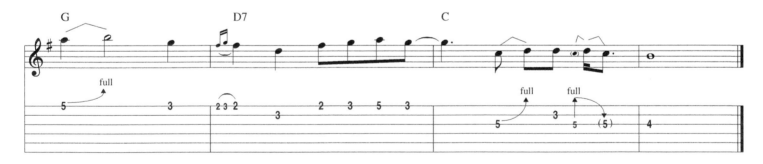

SUMMING UP—NOW YOU KNOW...

► *How to play three moveable major scales for each key*

► *How to play melodies in all keys in two or three registers*

► *How to ornament a major-scale-based melody*

♪ USING THE PRACTICE TRACKS

The roadmaps illuminate many soloing styles, including:

▶ *first position major scales*

▶ *chord fragment licks*

▶ *blues boxes*

▶ *substitute blues boxes*

▶ *sliding (major) pentatonic scales*

▶ *sliding scale double-note licks and steel licks*

▶ *moveable (1st & 3rd string) double-note licks*

▶ *moveable major scales*

On the five practice tracks, the lead guitar is separated from the rest of the band—it's on one side of your stereo. You can tune it out and use the band as backup, trying out any soloing techniques you like. You can also imitate the lead guitar; here are the soloing ideas on each track:

 #1 HONKY TONK GUITAR (in E)—The soloist plays first position E licks during this I–IV–I–V tune, and switches to first position A licks when the tune modulates to A.

 #2 CARELESS LOVE (in G)—You'll hear chord fragment licks during this country-rock tune, including 1st and 3rd string double-note licks. The first time around the tune, soloing is based on the F formation/G chord at the 3rd fret; the second time it's based on the D formation/G chord at the 7th fret; the third time it's based on the A formation/G chord at the 12th fret.

 #3 HONKY TONK #2 (in A)—The soloist uses a substitute (F♯) blues box during this I–IV–V progression, then switches to the three A blues boxes.

 #4 STAGOLEE (in G)—In this 12-bar blues, the solos are based on G, C and D sliding scales. There are steel licks, single-note and double-note licks.

 #5 REDWING (in G)—Moveable G major scales are the basis for the solos in this country classic.

Guitar Notation Legend

Guitar Music can be notated three different ways: on a *musical staff*, in *tablature*, and in *rhythm slashes*.

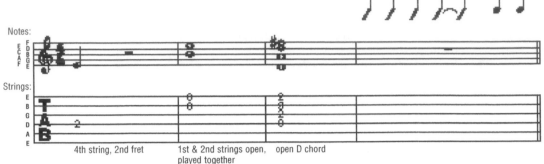

RHYTHM SLASHES are written above the staff. Strum chords in the rhythm indicated. Use the chord diagrams found at the top of the first page of the transcription for the appropriate chord voicings. Round noteheads indicate single notes.

THE MUSICAL STAFF shows pitches and rhythms and is divided by bar lines into measures. Pitches are named after the first seven letters of the alphabet.

TABLATURE graphically represents the guitar fingerboard. Each horizontal line represents a string, and each number represents a fret.

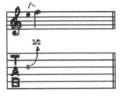

4th string, 2nd fret   1st & 2nd strings open, played together   open D chord

HALF-STEP BEND: Strike the note and bend up 1/2 step.

WHOLE-STEP BEND: Strike the note and bend up one step.

GRACE NOTE BEND: Strike the note and bend up as indicated. The first note does not take up any time.

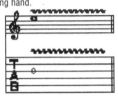

SLIGHT (MICROTONE) BEND: Strike the note and bend up 1/4 step.

BEND AND RELEASE: Strike the note and bend up as indicated, then release back to the original note. Only the first note is struck.

PRE-BEND: Bend the note as indicated, then strike it.

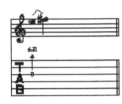

VIBRATO: The string is vibrated by rapidly bending and releasing the note with the fretting hand.

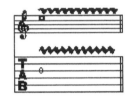

WIDE VIBRATO: The pitch is varied to a greater degree by vibrating with the fretting hand.

HAMMER-ON: Strike the first (lower) note with one finger, then sound the higher note (on the same string) with another finger by fretting it without picking.

PULL-OFF: Place both fingers on the notes to be sounded. Strike the first note and without picking, pull the finger off to sound the second (lower) note.

LEGATO SLIDE: Strike the first note and then slide the same fret-hand finger up or down to the second note. The second note is not struck.

SHIFT SLIDE: Same as legato slide, except the second note is struck.

TRILL: Very rapidly alternate between the notes indicated by continuously hammering on and pulling off.

TAPPING: Hammer ("tap") the fret indicated with the pick-hand index or middle finger and pull off to the note fretted by the fret hand.

NATURAL HARMONIC: Strike the note while the fret-hand lightly touches the string directly over the fret indicated.

PINCH HARMONIC: The note is fretted normally and a harmonic is produced by adding the edge of the thumb or the tip of the index finger of the pick hand to the normal pick attack.

PICK SCRAPE: The edge of the pick is rubbed down (or up) the string, producing a scratchy sound.

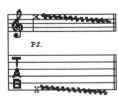

MUFFLED STRINGS: A percussive sound is produced by laying the fret hand across the string(s) without depressing, and striking them with the pick hand.

PALM MUTING: The note is partially muted by the pick hand lightly touching the string(s) just before the bridge.

RAKE: Drag the pick across the strings indicated with a single motion.

TREMOLO PICKING: The note is picked as rapidly and continuously as possible.

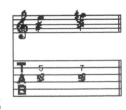

VIBRATO BAR DIVE AND RETURN: The pitch of the note or chord is dropped a specified number of steps (in rhythm) then returned to the original pitch.

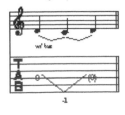

VIBRATO BAR SCOOP: Depress the bar just before striking the note, then quickly release the bar.

VIBRATO BAR DIP: Strike the note and then immediately drop a specified number of steps, then release back to the original pitch.

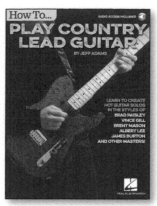
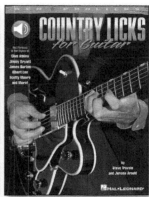

Guitar Instruction
Country Style!
from Hal Leonard

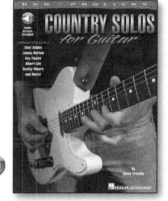

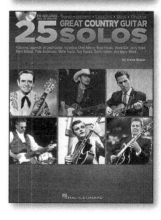

CHICKEN PICKIN' • *by Eric Halbig* INCLUDES TAB

This book provides a "bird's-eye-view" of the techniques and licks common to playing hot, country lead guitar! Covers over 100 hot country guitar licks: open-string licks, double-stop licks, scales, string bending, repetitive sequences, and chromatic licks. The online audio includes 99 demonstration tracks with each lick performed at two tempos.

00695599 Book/Online Audio...$17.99

DANIEL DONATO –
THE NEW MASTER OF THE TELECASTER INCLUDES TAB DVD

PATHWAYS TO DYNAMIC SOLOS

This exclusive instructional book and DVD set includes guitar lessons taught by young Nashville phenom Daniel Donato. The "New Master of the Telecaster" shows you his unique "pathways" concept, opening your mind and fingers to uninhibited fretboard freedom, increased music theory comprehension, and more dynamic solos! The DVD features Daniel Donato himself providing full-band performances and a full hour of guitar lessons. The book includes guitar tab for all the DVD lessons and performances. Topics covered include: using chromatic notes • application of bends • double stops • analyzing different styles • and more. DVD running time: 1 hr., 4 min.

00121923 Book/DVD Pack $19.99

FRETBOARD ROADMAPS – COUNTRY GUITAR INCLUDES TAB

The Essential Patterns That All the Pros Know and Use • by Fred Sokolow

This book/CD pack will teach you how to play lead and rhythm in the country style anywhere on the fretboard in any key. You'll play basic country progressions, boogie licks, steel licks, and other melodies and licks. You'll also learn a variety of lead guitar styles using moveable scale patterns, sliding scale patterns, chord-based licks, double-note licks, and more. The book features easy-to-follow diagrams and instructions for beginning, intermediate, and advanced players.

00695353 Book/CD Pack...$15.99

HOW TO PLAY COUNTRY LEAD GUITAR INCLUDES TAB

by Jeff Adams

Here is a comprehensive stylistic breakdown of country guitar techniques from the past 50 years. Drawing inspiration from the timelessly innovative licks of Merle Travis, Chet Atkins, Albert Lee, Vince Gill, Brent Mason and Brad Paisley, the near 90 musical examples within these pages will hone your left and right hands with technical string-bending and rolling licks while sharpening your knowledge of the thought process behind creating your own licks, and why and when to play them.

00131103 Book/Online Audio...$19.99

COUNTRY LICKS FOR GUITAR INCLUDES TAB

by Steve Trovato and Jerome Arnold

This unique package examines the lead guitar licks of the masters of country guitar, such as Chet Atkins, Jimmy Bryant, James Burton, Albert Lee, Scotty Moore, and many others! The online audio includes demonstrations of each lick at normal and slow speeds. The instruction covers single-string licks, pedal-steel licks, open-string licks, chord licks, rockabilly licks, funky country licks, tips on fingerings, phrasing, technique, theory, and application.

00695577 Book/Online Audo...........................$17.99

COUNTRY SOLOS
FOR GUITAR INCLUDES TAB

by Steve Trovato

This unique book/audio pack lets guitarists examine the solo styles of axe masters such as Chet Atkins, James Burton, Ray Flacke, Albert Lee, Scotty Moore, Roy Nichols, Jerry Reed and others. It covers techniques including hot banjo rolls, funky double stops, pedal-steel licks, open-string licks and more, in standard notation and tab with phrase-by-phrase performance notes. The online audio includes full demonstrations and rhythm-only tracks.

00695448 Book/Online Audio...........................$17.99

RED-HOT COUNTRY GUITAR

by Michael Hawley

The complete guide to playing lead guitar in the styles of Pete Anderson, Danny Gatton, Albert Lee, Brent Mason, and more. Includes loads of red-hot licks, techniques, solos, theory and more.

00695831 Book/Online Audio...$17.99

25 GREAT COUNTRY GUITAR SOLOS INCLUDES TAB

by Dave Rubin

Provides solo transcriptions in notes & tab, lessons on how to play them, guitarist bios, equipment notes, photos, history, and much more. The CD contains full-band demos of every solo in the book. Songs include: Country Boy • Foggy Mountain Special • Folsom Prison Blues • Hellecaster Theme • Hello Mary Lou • I've Got a Tiger by the Tail • The Only Daddy That Will Walk the Line • Please, Please Baby • Sugarfoot Rag • and more.

00699926 Book/CD Pack...$19.99